7 DAY

PRAYER CHALLENGE

Becoming Consistent, Committed and Faithful in Prayer

ERICA WILLIAMS

7-DAY PRAYER CHALLENGE
Copyright © 2020 Erica Williams

All rights reserved. Printed in the United States of America. No part of this book may be used or reproduced in any manner whatsoever without written permission except in the case of brief quotations in critical articles or reviews.

Unless otherwise noted, all Bible quotations are from the King James Version of the Bible.

Cover Design, Typesetting, Book Layout by
Enger Lanier Taylor for In Due Season Publishing

Published By: In Due Season Publishing
               Huntsville, Alabama
               indueseasonpublishing@gmail.com

www.indueseasonpublishing.com
ISBN-13:   978-1-970057-08-9
ISBN-10:   1-970057-08-4

www.meetingwiththemastermin2020@gmail.com
Facebook Search: Erica Williams
Instagram: heartofanintercessor_2015 /Twitter: Miss.Sunshine
Periscope: PastorE2020
Email: thoughtsofanintercessor2020@gmail.com

Disclaimer:
The information provided in this book is designed to provide helpful information. This book is not meant to be used, nor should it be used, to diagnose, treat or advise in the area of fasting and any of your medical conditions. For diagnosis or treatment of any medical problem, consult your own physician. The publisher and author are not responsible for any specific health or allergy needs that may require medical supervision and are not liable for any damages or negative consequences from any treatment, action, application or preparation, to any person reading or following the information in this book.

CONTENTS

Day 1 10
Facing the Truth & Being Vulnerable

Day 2 13
Setting Time of Prayer

Day 3 16
What does it mean to be Consistent, Committed & Faithful

Day 4 20
Fasting & Prayer

Day 5 24
Consistent, Committed and Faithful to Prayer

Day 6 27
My Purpose

Day 7 31
What's Next God?

About The Author..37

Introduction

What is a Challenge?
A challenge is an invitation, summons, or call to enter into a confrontation or test.

What in the world is this 7-Day Prayer Challenge really about? I challenge you to keep reading and surrender to being more consistent, committed, and faithful to prayer and building your relationship with the Lord. I know you may be wondering now how did this become about me? Well, it's no mistake, the Lord is speaking, and He wants to talk to you. Sometimes as believers, we make stuff so deep. Prayer, in its simplest form, is talking to God. I want to let you in on a little secret; the Lord wants your time and attention. It is an honor and privilege that the creator of Heaven and Earth, the self-sustaining One, is inviting us to the table for one on one time.

Hmmm, are you still asking……. Why did I even pick this up? You may even think you don't need a prayer challenge. I can hear some saying; I am an intercessor and a prayer warrior. I pray all the time. I already know that.

7-DAY PRAYER CHALLENGE

That may be true, but have you truly been faithful, committed, and consistent with your prayer life today (Thessalonians 5:17)? Just because we are doing something, every day does not mean that we are consistent, faithful, and committed in a way that will produce change, growth, and maturity (Matthew 6:7).

I know some pick up this prayer challenge and journal up who just gave their life to the Lord and are a little nervous about prayer. I have good news. God wants to not only hear from you but talk to you. He thinks you are pretty special. He has a plan and purpose for your life. Yes, you. Do not be afraid, scared, or nervous because you are thinking about your past. God is not focused on your past. He's ready to establish a firm foundation. He forgave you when you accepted Jesus Christ as your personal Lord and Savior. You are special, wanted, needed, and necessary. What better time than now to develop a prayer life? Take a deep breath. Remember, this is between you and God. My dear sister or brother, I can see you are thinking about how your mother, friend, or Pastor prays. Take another deep breath; you don't have to pray like them. God created us all different and unique. Your prayer time and relationship with the Lord is just as valuable as anyone else in the entire world. This challenge for you is a two-fold blessing. You will get insight into what happens to a lot of us, and now you can avoid these pitfalls.

Over the last 20 years of being in church and being a part of ministries, when there is a decline, I have noticed that the first thing to go is our prayer lives. We get so busy with the work of the ministry, family, finances, relationships, business, and moving fast that we forget to spend that quality time needed and necessary in prayer and communion with the Father. Prayer once was a priority. We took joy in spending time in prayer. We were a living witness that God answered our prayers. (James 5:16). Think about it; everything that you have become was birthed out of prayer. Let's be honest with our selves. We used to attend prayer meetings and were excited to spend time in prayer. We set aside a time in the morning, and we even had a special meeting place for prayer (Psalm 63:1).

Yet, the business of life kicked in, and we started to short change God and give Him the bare minimum. It went from quality to quantity. It goes from being a big deal like going on a hot date to a 5-star restaurant to going through the drive-through at a fast food restaurant. It has become common and familiar. We start treating our prayer time and prayer life like it's no longer important as it used to be. We begin to make excuses and become lazy. Once we start getting in our flesh and not keeping prayer on the top of our "to do" list, our relationship with the Lord becomes boring and stagnant. We begin to treat God like a genie in the bottle or Santa Claus.

When this happens, our relationship becomes more distant and broken. We don't recognize His voice like we once did, and it changes our vision and the decisions we make. We begin only to have "911" personal prayer time. When we were consistent, committed, and faithful in prayer, we heard everything God said. We received our plans and strategies for our day to day lives, family, job, ministry, business, and finances in prayer.

Our relationship with the father is not disposable. When we treat it like a drive-through, that's the mentality that we take on. We must remember that our time of prayer is special every time. God never gives us leftovers and gives us his attention and best (Lamentations 3:22-23). Spending time in prayer is like going to a fancy restaurant. There aren't any paper plates, plastic spoons, or cheap napkins at the table of the Lord, and nothing is discarded. Your time with Him will be well spent and is worth the investment.

God serves us with a spirit of excellence. He is perfect in all His ways. At the table, with the Lord, we get to eat the best of food on fine china. Everything about the table of the Lord is beautiful and priceless. We don't only get natural benefits of prayer but spiritual benefits. We get a 66 book menu that is filled with all the things that will give us abundant life.

Our relationship with the Lord is the most important relationship we can have and will benefit our other relationships as well. Prayer sets the tone. The first step is admitting we need HELP in prayer and building our relationship.

There is nothing wrong with admitting when we need help. Acknowledging that need helps to kill pride and opens the door for humility to develop. The Lord is ready and willing to help us every day. God is relational. He's a communicator. God speaks in all of our love languages and desires to have a relationship with each of us (John 3:16). It's an honor to have the creator of Heaven and Earth desire to have a relationship with us. We are a big deal to him. The more we spend time in prayer, the stronger our relationship grows, and the wiser we become. We will begin to seek Him on everything and not just some things. We can be vulnerable with God. and can come boldly before the throne of Grace. We can be naked and unashamed because He will not condemn us, but correct us in love. Then heal us, grow us up, and send us out to expand the Kingdom of God. There is nothing like God's scent on us. There is something amazing about the light of Christ shining and the glory of the Lord resting upon us. We begin to look like him.

Yes, you may be praying regularly, but are you actively listening to what the Lord is saying? Are you taking notes and getting your marching orders? Sometimes we become overly spiritual or even religious with God in prayer. Prayer is a two-way conversation and requires us to listen just as much as talk. We need to be quick to hear and slow to speak (James 1:19).

A person can lay hands on you every day and declare that you are an intercessor or prayer warrior. But until you submit to private prayer and focus on being consistent, committed, and faithful, it is in vain. Prayer can be viewed as a contact sport; meaning this is hands on. Jesus is our best teacher, and He shows us by example. He even questioned the disciples about not being able to pray for an hour (Matthew 26:40).

I can pray at the drop of a hat, but even after all this time, I still need to be more consistent, committed, and faithful to prayer. Prayer is not seasonal, or a fad and is always trending. We must be intentional. Sometimes we get caught in the hype of different books concerning prayer and try to mimic them. Our prayer life cannot be lived vicariously through anyone else. We have to put in the work and develop a one on one prayer relationship with God.

This challenge is the beginning to jump start or reset you. This will challenge you to be more purpose driven. Prayer is exciting yet can be labor intensive in the beginning, but the rewards are a closer relationship with the Lord, and a firm foundation built to withstand the test of time.

Special Messages to Leaders

Leaders, hear my heart as a daughter and intercessor for over twenty years. What I witnessed was a lot of leaders, especially senior leaders of local churches who have people who are always praying for them. They eventually get to a place where they pass prayer on to others in the ministry and step away entirely from the ministry of prayer. I'm a firm believer, that if prayer is not important to you, it will not be important to the sheep. We must lead by example.

I've seen many leaders attempt to preach prayer, but prayer must be taught. Jesus was the best teacher of prayer. He not only taught it, but he demonstrated it. The Lord's Prayer is our model. We can pass the baton to have a son or daughter in the ministry to be over the prayer ministry, but don't stop being the lead servant in prayer in the house. Children need to see parents praying. The Lord said to make houses of prayer.

7-DAY PRAYER CHALLENGE

I'm so grateful that you have agreed to take this *7-Day Prayer Challenge*. What is a challenge? A challenge is an invitation, summons, or call to enter into a confrontation or test. It means to arise, stimulate, or jump start. A challenge may be a difficult task, often painful, and always demanding. A challenge is what makes the true value, beauty, and fulfillment possible. Challenges can be tough, yet indeed it brings about a change and greater understanding of a thing (Merriam-Webster Dictionary).

I'm so proud of each of you. You are making a bold statement of faith. I believe that over the next seven days, your prayer life and relationship with the Lord is going to grow, and you will be sharpened. He has a desire to talk and commune with you. Building a foundation takes work. Challenges come, but you are victorious and an overcomer (Philippians 4:13). Remember, you are stepping out by faith for the next seven days. The Bible says that the just shall live by faith (Romans 1:17).

SURRENDER!	(Romans 12:1,6)
SUBMIT!	(James 4:7-10)
OBEY!	(1 Samuel 15:22-24)

7-DAY PRAYER CHALLENGE

AGREEMENT

I_____agree to be consistent, committed and faithful to prayer for the next 7 days. I submit to_____ and agree that they are given permission to hold me accountable.

Date:_____
Signature:_____
Signature:_____

Matthew 18:19
Again, truly I tell you that if two of you on earth agree about anything they ask for, it will be done for them by my Father in Heaven.

Proverbs 27:17
As iron sharpens iron, so one person sharpens another.

Ecclesiastes 4:9-12
Two are better than one, because they have a good return for their labor:[10] If either of them falls down one can help the other up. But pity anyone who falls and has no one to help them up.[11] Also, if two lie down together, they will keep warm. But how can one keep warm alone?[12] Though one may be overpowered, two can defend themselves. A cord of three strands is not quickly broken.

DAY 1

Facing the Truth and Being Vulnerable With God

It's not always easy to face the truth about ourselves, to be vulnerable and open up. But we must be determined our past does not have to keep us from having a healthy relationship with the Lord. He gave His only begotten son so that we can have eternal life. We are forgiven. We have been redeemed. We have been saved through the blood of Christ Jesus. God can be trusted with our weakness, fragilities, flaws, and imperfections. God's love is unconditional. He has already forgiven us and thrown our sins into the sea of forgetfulness. God is a good Father. He protects, keeps, sustains, provides, and loves us beyond our wildest dreams. God is faithful. God is not a man that He should lie. Go ahead and open up to the Father. Look in the mirror, open up your mouth, and admit you desire to be more consistent, committed, and faithful to prayer and building your relationship with Him.

You have already taken the first step by reading the above and signing off on the agreement to being open and honest about needing to be more consistent, faithful, and

7-DAY PRAYER CHALLENGE

committed to prayer. Now let's move forward in this challenge. Please sign the agreement form and have your accountability partner sign as well. Declare that pride dies, and humility is resuscitated & resurrected.

Special Note

Over the next seven days, journaling will be essential.

Remember, if you get stuck/want to change your mind to:

✓Call upon the name of Jesus.
✓Cry out for HELP! (Psalm 91:15)
✓PRAY IN THE HOLY GHOST! (Ephesians 6:18)

_____
_____
_____
_____
_____
_____
_____
_____
_____
_____
_____
_____
_____
_____
_____
_____
_____
_____

7-DAY PRAYER CHALLENGE

DAY 2

Setting a Time In Prayer

Set specific times of prayer every morning and evening. Pray at these times each day and ask God to show you what is hindering you and your prayer life. Repent! Ask for forgiveness! Expect to hear from the Lord. Ask the Lord to open your eyes and heart to reveal the hidden things that need to be dealt with. Be open to healing and deliverance because it is the children's bread. He is our chief physician, and stabilizer, so don't let your feelings and emotions get in the way. Receive by faith and depend upon the Holy Spirit.

- ✓ Remember to take notes
- ✓ Don't rush into prayer.
- ✓ Be still!
- ✓ Be open to receiving from the Lord.
- ✓ Be vulnerable because He loves you.
- ✓ The Lord speaks to us in different ways, yet it will always be according to His Word.
- ✓ Don't be surprised if he speaks to you during the day.

7-DAY PRAYER CHALLENGE

It's called a CHALLENGE on PURPOSE! You got this!

7-DAY PRAYER CHALLENGE

DAY 3

Research The Following

✓ Consistent
✓ Faithful
✓ Committed

Write down what you find in your journal. Sometimes we don't know the actual meaning of a word. Dig deep while getting a true definition of what each one means. I've learned that we may think we're doing something, but in reality, it's just in our thoughts.

Now talk to the Father in prayer about embracing all three in your personal relationship and prayer life.

*Go to the Word of God and find one scripture that you can stand on for each word; **consistent, faithful**, and **commitment**,

7-DAY PRAYER CHALLENGE

REMEMBER:
NO CONDEMNATION (Romans 8:1)
NO SHAME (Romans 10:11)
NO EXCUSE (Philippians 4:13)

It is called a challenge on purpose; for a purpose! If you get stuck, let your accountability partner know and use your weapons.

- Call on the name of JESUS
- HELP- Ask Him for it
- PRAY IN THE HOLY GHOST (stir yourself up)

_____
_____
_____
_____
_____
_____
_____
_____
_____
_____
_____
_____
_____
_____
_____
_____
_____

7-DAY PRAYER CHALLENGE

7-DAY PRAYER CHALLENGE

DAY 4

Fasting

Good morning my dear sisters and brothers. I hope that you are well, yet being challenged. I pray that you are being blessed in your time of studying what being faithful, committed, and consistent means today on your journey.

Don't forget to take notes in your journal.

Day four is a day of fasting. Yes, I said fasting! I heard Him say, This kind goes out by fasting and praying (Matthew 17:21). He has even more to say to you. Some of you may be taking medication and need to consult your physician regarding any type of fast that you will participate in. You must use wisdom (*See Disclaimer*).

You will fast from 6:00 am to 6:00 pm and may drink water, 100% juice, or hot tea. CHALLENGE & SACRIFICE! When you come off the fast in the evening, eat a light dinner and close your night off with prayer.

Find three examples of fasting in the Bible and write them

in your journal. I truly believe and look forward to hearing the powerful testimonies and praise reports that will be coming after these seven days.

I took this challenge also, and on the fourth day, I found myself weeping before the Lord for each of you who would take the challenge. I couldn't stop thanking the Lord for all He is doing and getting ready to do. It's no mistake that you are participating in this challenge, and I believe that as a result, your relationship with God will grow. Use this as a time of preparation for what is to come. God has a purpose for everything.

I saw breakthrough and restoration taking place for you; strongholds destroyed; and I heard that we shall recover all. I saw the waters of life that tried to drown you beginning to recede. The good news is you are anchored in the Lord. JESUS.. We all are being challenged and held accountable to obeying God. Prophecy is being fulfilled.

_____
_____
_____
_____
_____
_____
_____
_____
_____

7-DAY PRAYER CHALLENGE

7-DAY PRAYER CHALLENGE

DAY 5

Did You Complete Yesterday's Challenge?

Fasting 6 am to 6 pm.

Today's challenge is that you find **a man** and **woman** of the Bible who was **consistent, committed, and faithful** to prayer and take notes on what you can learn from their life and journey. Choose one from the old testament and one from the new testament. Jesus is the only one that is off limits. That's too easy.

This challenge was designed to make you stronger and wiser. NO EXCUSES! We in this together FOR REAL!

I will continue to say that all things are working together for your good. Don't allow the enemy to make you think that God is not listening, helping, and responding to you. He's watching over His word to perform it (Jeremiah 1:12). You matter to God, and He is mindful of you (Psalm 8:3-5). Don't get weary in well doing (Galatians 6:9). Stop overthinking or intellectualizing this challenge and finish. The opposition is a part of warfare, but Heaven is backing you up.

You are being prayed for every day (Hebrews 7:25). If you didn't fast yesterday. The number five is the number of grace, so pray and fast again today.

Please write in your journal and be honest with yourself on what happened and what hindered you. Remember you are safe in God. This is not a gotcha slipping or about condemnation. It is about being transparent on this journey with the Lord.

_____
_____
_____
_____
_____
_____
_____
_____
_____
_____
_____
_____
_____
_____

7-DAY PRAYER CHALLENGE

DAY 6

Write down in your journal what your purpose and call are. If you don't know, ask God! Then write down how you are going to be more consistent, faithful, and committed to your call and purpose. Just for the record, you can have a call and purpose in the marketplace also.

Of course, you should be still praying at the same time in the morning and evening as well as writing in your journal what you hear the Lord sharing with you about you. If you have been struggling the last two days with fasting Day 6 is another opportunity to do it 6 am to 6 pm (liquids only unless you are under a doctors care and/or taking medicine.. see disclaimer)

Nine types of prayers are demonstrated and/or talked about in the Bible.

Describe............
- What is the prayer of faith (James 5:15)
- What is the prayer of agreement (also known as corporate prayer) (Acts 2:42)
- What is a prayer of request (also known as petition

7-DAY PRAYER CHALLENGE

or supplication) (Philippians 4:6)
- What is a prayer of thanksgiving (Psalm 95:2-3)
- What is a prayer of worship (Acts 13:2-3)
- What is a prayer of consecration (also known as dedication) (Matthew 26:39)
- What is a prayer of intercession (1 Timothy 2:1)
- What is a prayer of imprecation (Psalms 69)
- What is praying in the Spirit (1 Corinthians 14:14-15).

CHALLENGE..................NO EXCUSES.......... You are victorious.

7-DAY PRAYER CHALLENGE

You have reached the final day. I pray that your relationship with the Lord continues to grow, and you are now more consistent, faithful, and committed in praying and building your relationship with the Lord. I pray you take what He has revealed about you and use the opportunity to grow and mature in Jesus' name.

DAY 7

Pray at the times that you already set in place. Ask God what's next/new? Write down everything He says and be honest with what you hear. Feel free to email me to share your experience, praise reports, and testimonies to meetingwiththemastermin2020@gmail.com

7-DAY PRAYER CHALLENGE

7-DAY PRAYER CHALLENGE

7-DAY PRAYER CHALLENGE

<u>Trivia</u>

Do you know how many prayers are mentioned in the Bible (and how many were answered)? Here's the answer to that question and other things you should know about prayer in the Bible.

1. There are 650 prayers listed in the Bible.

2. There are approximately 450 recorded answers to prayer in the Bible.

3. The first time prayer is mentioned in the Bible is Genesis 4:26 (earlier dialogues were initiated directly by God, e.g., Genesis 3:8-13, Genesis 4:9).

4. The Bible records Jesus praying 25 different times during his earthly ministry.

5. In the Bible, Paul mentions prayer (prayers, prayer reports, prayer requests, exhortations to pray), 41 times.

6. Although prayer can (and should) be done from any bodily position, the Bible lists five specific postures:
- Sitting (2 Sam 7:18)
- Standing (Mark 11:25)
- Kneeling (Chronicles 6:13; Daniel 6:10; Luke 22:41; Acts 7:60, 9:40, 20:36, 21:5; Ephesians 3:14)
- With one's face to the ground (Matthew 26:39; Mark 14:35)
- With hands lifted up (1 Timothy 2:8).

7. The Bible lists five areas of focus in prayer (Luke 11:1-4):
    - God's name be honored – the focus on His everlasting glory ("Father, hallowed be your name")
    - God's Kingdom come – the focus on his eternal will ("your kingdom come")
    - God's provision is given – the focus on our present ("Give us each day our daily bread.")
    - God's forgiveness is granted – the focus on our past (Forgive us our sins, for we also forgive everyone who sins against us.)
    - God's deliverance will be provided – the focus on our future.

8. The Bible lists at least nine main types of prayer:
    - Prayer of Faith (James 5:15)
    - Prayer of Agreement- also known as corporate prayer (Acts 2:42)
    - Prayer of request - also known as petition or supplication (Philippians 4:6)
    - Prayer of Thanksgiving (Psalm 95:2-3)
    - Prayer of worship (Acts 13:2-3)
    - Prayer of Consecration - also known as dedication (Matthew 26:39)
    - Prayer of Intercession (1 Timothy 2:1)
    - Prayer of Imprecation (Psalms 69)
    - Praying in the Spirit (1 Corinthians 14:14-15)

9. The word "amen" (which means "let it be, "so be it," "verily," "truly") makes its first appearance in the Bible in Numbers

5:22. In that passage, God commands it to be said by a person who is yielding to his examination.

7-DAY PRAYER CHALLENGE

NOTES

7-DAY PRAYER CHALLENGE

NOTES

7-DAY PRAYER CHALLENGE

NOTES

//7-DAY PRAYER CHALLENGE

NOTES

7-DAY PRAYER CHALLENGE

NOTES

7-DAY PRAYER CHALLENGE

NOTES

7-DAY PRAYER CHALLENGE

NOTES

7-DAY PRAYER CHALLENGE

NOTES

7-DAY PRAYER CHALLENGE

NOTES

7-DAY PRAYER CHALLENGE

NOTES

7-DAY PRAYER CHALLENGE

NOTES

… 7-DAY PRAYER CHALLENGE

NOTES

7-DAY PRAYER CHALLENGE

NOTES

7-DAY PRAYER CHALLENGE

NOTES _____

7-DAY PRAYER CHALLENGE

NOTES_____

7-DAY PRAYER CHALLENGE

NOTES _____

ABOUT THE AUTHOR

Pastor Erica L. Williams has been in ministry for over twenty years. She received the call on her life as an intercessor early on in ministry. Pastor Erica was ordained and licensed as a Pastor in April of 2014. Pastor Erica is also the founder of *Meeting with the Master Ministries.* Her mission is to train, teach, and share the importance and value of prayer. Pastor Erica has a unique style in activating and equipping the body of Christ to help strengthen and elevate their communication with God.

She is very passionate about sharing the importance of building your relationship with the Lord while walking in the fruit of the spirit. Her love for people and seeing them empowered through prayer has always been the focal point of her ministry. She believes in the power of prayer and has been a witness to God's miracles and power being displayed through believers. Pastor E, as she is affectionately known, has worked in workforce development for over seventeen years, ten of those years were spent working with youth. She has a BS Degree from Southern Illinois University and currently attends Restoring the Walls Church, where she is an Associate Pastor. She takes joy in spending time with family and friends. Pastor Erica is honored to wear the hat of Auntie Erica to three nieces and two nephews and to be called daughter by her mother, Ethel Williams. Erica has three sisters and enjoys spending quality time with family and friends. In her downtime, you will find her taking a road trip or sitting by a lake, river, or ocean. It is her place of serenity.

Salvation

As a Pastor, it is my duty to make sure I offer salvation to anyone who picks up this book. If you were to die today, are you sure you are going to Heaven? No need to fret; if you answered no, all you have to do is, Confess with your mouth Jesus is Lord, believe in your heart that He was raised from the dead, and accept Him in your life. If you read that and agree with it, you are now born again. Heaven and the angels rejoice when a new soul is won to the Kingdom of Heaven (Romans 10:9-10).

www.ingramcontent.com/pod-product-compliance
Lightning Source LLC
Chambersburg PA
CBHW071242090426
42736CB00014B/3186